THE S GPA™

MAWI ASGEDOM
AUTHOR OF "OF BEETLES & ANGELS"

Table of Contents

Introduction

Paul had a learning disability called dyslexia that made it difficult for him to read. As Paul describes it, sentences looked like Egyptian hieroglyphics.

After failing second grade, Paul was put in a class for developmentally challenged kids. He was expelled from four different schools and graduated from high school ranked 1192 out of 1200 students.

Another student, Mandy Stephens, got straight A's in high school. Her counselor recommended she apply to top colleges. Mandy attended Harvard University and earned three Harvard degrees – her undergraduate, her masters, and her doctorate.

Paul went on to start a chain of copy centers called Kinko's. He eventually sold the company to FedEx for 2.4 billion dollars! How's that for a kid who failed second grade?

Although Mandy had three degrees from Harvard, at age thirty-one, she was unemployed and had to live with her parents. Mandy knew how to get A's, but she did not have much self-confidence. She froze up in job interviews, and after being rejected a few times, she felt so defeated that she stopped applying.

The point of these two stories is not that grades don't matter. Grades matter. Colleges look at your Grade Point Average (GPA) and your test scores to decide whether you will be admitted. One day, employers will consider your educational background before they hire you. Grades are also one measure of your skill in writing, reading, and math.

But as Paul's story shows, you are more than your grades.

Let's take a closer look at how Paul made it through college.

Paul's college assigned a lot of reading, and Paul quickly fell hopelessly behind. Instead of dropping out, Paul formed study groups with his classmates. Paul did all the extra things like photocopying when the group needed it, and setting up the meeting times. In return, the group helped Paul by explaining the readings to him.

What was Paul doing? He was using the strengths of others to succeed. Paul discovered that knowing how to get "A" students to work with you is even more powerful than being the "A" student. What else was Paul doing? He was solving his problem. Instead of feeling sorry for himself, Paul found a way to graduate.

What if, like Paul, you had power and ability that could not be measured by your grades? What if you could develop your non-academic "power" to help yourself succeed?

The Success GPA

Whether you are an A-student or barely scraping by, you have abilities that your report card cannot measure. Your normal GPA measures your performance in things like math and history. In contrast, your Success GPA looks at the key non-academic skills that drive success.

The Success GPA has three parts called "powers" because they increase your capacity to achieve in all areas of life:

1// Awareness Power: Do you know yourself? Can you use your unique personality, your strengths and weaknesses, and your "self-understanding" to make good decisions?

2// Social Power: Can you connect with others? Can you create a powerful social network that helps you and others?

3// Solution Power: Can you solve real-life problems? Can you tackle difficult challenges and create lasting solutions?

Together, your Awareness, Connection, and Solution powers form your Success GPA.

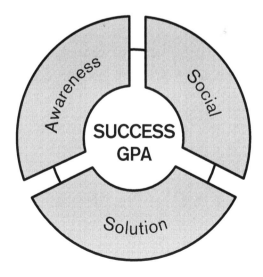

Here are some situations where the Success GPA matters:

1// You want to go on a spring break trip that costs $750, but you only have $50 in the bank. Your parents don't have any extra money to give you.

2// You think you should start on your softball team, but the coach refuses to give you a chance.

3// Your freshman year of college, you realize the roommate you were assigned to is a real pain.

These three situations are quite common, and yet finding a solution will not come from having a high grade in math.

For example, let's see what happened with Carlie, the student with the difficult roommate. Within two weeks, Carlie realized that her roommate Jen's behavior was inconsiderate and a bit out of control. Jen played loud music until 4:30 AM every night, borrowed Carlie's clothes without asking, and kept food in the room until it grew green fungus. Carlie talked to Jen and she said she would change. But nothing happened.

How did Carlie solve this problem? Carlie had made friends with the people two floors below her, and when one of their roommates suddenly had to leave school, Carlie asked if she could move in. They said yes, which meant goodbye to Jen the bad roommate!

Like Carlie, you can use your Social Power to help you get a new roommate, a new job, or a new date. But if all you do is study alone in your room, when you have a problem like an annoying roommate, you'll be stuck.

The Success GPA™ is based on work with more than 1,000,000 students in 40 states. Ongoing research with college students shows that having a high Success GPA increases the chances of getting a job, avoiding credit card debt, graduating from college on time, and many other positive results.

Your Success GPA

In 2002, Fortune Magazine ran a cover story describing that many successful CEOs struggled in school just like Paul did. As adults, these successful CEOs viewed their classroom problems as advantages, because the CEOs were forced to develop non-academic skills.

How about you? What would it mean for you to develop strong non-academic skills that you could use throughout your life? If you're the kind of person who gets great grades easily, how are you doing with your Success GPA? Can you solve real-life problems? Do you have a strong social network? Do you understand your strengths and weaknesses?

Maybe you're like Paul, and you struggle in school. Don't give up. Keep doing your best in your regular classes, and realize the Success GPA gives you an extra way to win.

In the coming pages, you'll learn how to develop each part of the Success GPA. Each of the three sections – Awareness, Social, and Solution – has three parts, so you'll learn a total of nine different ways to build your Success GPA.

As you're reading, keep one thing in mind: For most of the 1800's and 1900's, factory jobs drove the American economy. The main skill required to get these factory jobs was the ability to hit a button again and again.

Today, many of those factory jobs have gone to China or India. The jobs that are left – the good ones anyway – require you to work with others, solve problems, and understand your own strengths and weaknesses. Instead of working at a factory, you are the factory. Instead of assembly lines and machines, your workplace is your knowledge and skills.

Your classes and schoolwork give you one important way to build your "mental" factory. Combine your academic skills with The Success GPA™ and you will give yourself incredible power to shape your future.

Mawi
Asgedom

introduction

Chapter One

Awareness Power

Take a close look at this image.

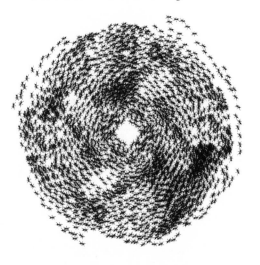

This is a picture of ants marching in a circle. These ants will keep following each other until they die – it's called a circular mill. Why do these ants keep marching? Because the ants do not have the ability to think about what they are doing.

As human beings, we are not the biggest, strongest, or fastest animals. But we have one key advantage: we can step back, think about what we are doing, and make changes to our behavior. This ability to think about our lives is called Awareness.

If you have high Awareness, you can:

// **Save yourself from yourself.** Max knew he was addicted
to a video game called Civilization. If it was on his hard
drive, he would play it every day for hours. Before he went
to college, Max deleted Civilization so it couldn't take over
his freshman year.

// **Adjust your thoughts in real-time.** You can stop yourself
in the middle of the day and ask, "How am I viewing this
situation? Do I need to change my attitude?" Or, you can
go on auto-pilot, and march on like the ants.

// **Improve social interactions.** Everyone, including you, is
wired differently. Some people are bubbly, giving a hug a
minute. Others are reserved; they would rather keep
hugging to a minimum. Wouldn't it be good to know who
you are, and to understand those around you?

Awareness does not mean that you know everything about
yourself. Awareness does mean that you pay attention to
how you think and make adjustments that have a big impact.
You will learn three ways to develop Awareness: **Talents,
Allocation,** and **Focus.**

// TALENT

As kids, most of us are taught a narrow definition for talent. We look at musicians like Alicia Keys and say, "Wow! She has so much talent!" We look at someone who can paint well and wish we had their talent.

Let's think back to Paul, who failed second grade but went on to start a billion dollar company. He wasn't a supreme athlete or an incredible artist, but he was talented. His talents included: (1) making friends (2) thinking creatively about problems, and (3) persevering in the face of challenges.

Talent is not just how high you jump or how well you paint. A talent is a strength or way of thinking that comes easy to you. For example, you might naturally enjoy asking lots of questions – you're very curious. You could become a great doctor with that talent because you'd know how to ask patients the right questions. Or, you could dislike talking to people, but enjoy working alone on math equations – you might become a great computer programmer.

You are different from everyone else, so there's no point in trying to do the same thing that your friend does or your older brother does. By developing awareness of your Talents, you can position yourself for success in any environment and figure out what will work best for you. You can unveil your blind spots and build teams with people who have talents that balance you out.

The best way to learn about your Talents is to focus on two areas: your unique Personality and your Strengths.

Personality

"Why must I be surrounded by idiots?" Have you ever asked yourself that question when you were working in a group? It can sometimes seem like 75% of people don't quite get it. They say stuff that makes you think, "On what planet does what he's saying make sense?"

Meanwhile, you seem to love working with the remaining 25%. You might think: "This girl knows what's up. She just gets it." You click with each other and have really exciting conversations where you can practically finish each other's sentences.

It turns out the 75% of people you might think are idiots are really just different from you. They have different personalities, which mean their minds just naturally generate thoughts that would never have occurred to you. The 25% you may have thought were geniuses are just people who are like you. It's fun to feel that agreement and connection with them, but you may be missing out on some new perspectives.

One way to understand personality is to think about which hand you like to write with. Some people are left-handed and some are right-handed. Neither one is wrong, but you definitely have a preference. To illustrate this point, try the activity described below.

// Activity //

Sign your name with your preferred hand. If you're right-handed, just sign your name as you always do with your right hand. (If you're left-handed, do the same, but with your left hand.) Now, sign your name with your other hand. How'd that feel? Was it weird? Most people report a similar experience. They get the job done either way; their name is on the paper. However, using the less-preferred hand tends to feel really awkward, takes much longer to finish, and looks like scribbles from a four-year-old.

Again, neither way is right or wrong, just different. Personality is the same way.

Let's take a look at a way to split people's personalities into four types. If you had to pick one, which one sounds most like you? It's okay if your personality seems to fall into more than one category. Just select the category that describes how you are most of the time.

Harmonizer	Organizer	Philosopher	Explorer
Sensitive	Directing	Analytical	Impulsive
Engaging	Stable	Rational	Competitive
Encouraging	Organized	Serious	Self-confident
Loving	Structured	Inquisitive	Proactive
Idealistic	Dependable	Intellectual	Curious
Kind	Detail-oriented	Visionary	Easygoing

Understanding your basic personality can help you comprehend why some people react differently to the same situations. Take a look at how different personalities might respond to these scenarios using the table on the next page:

Situation	Harmonizer	Organizer	Philosopher	Explorer
You get a bad grade on a major assignment.	Commiserates with other students who also received bad grades.	Takes careful note of each question that she missed and thinks through the correct answer.	Identifies the pattern in the questions he missed, in order to review the sections of the book that he understood least.	Focuses his efforts on another subject that's more interesting.
You're not invited to a party you really wanted to attend.	Feels sad or depressed; seeks out a close friend to hang out that night.	Uses the time to organize her music collection.	Thinks deeply about the underlying reasons for why he wasn't invited.	Checks out a movie she's been dying to see that no one else seemed interested in.
You're grounded.	Tries to use the phone, Facebook, or whatever means possible to stay con-nected to friends.	Studies hard at home so he can have more fun when released.	Writes down a ton of random, great ideas while under house arrest.	Finds some totally wild fungus growing in the attic.
Someone makes fun of you.	Shares with the person how the teasing made her feel and tries to repair the relationship.	Crosses that person off his friend list and plans to spend more time with quality friends.	Thinks through plenty of great insults to "get back at him" later.	Seeks out new friends.

awareness
power

Depending on which personality type describes you, certain things are more likely to aggravate you than others. So, keep these in mind:

// If you're a harmonizer, you are more likely to cringe at conflict and feel a knot in your stomach at the thought of telling someone that he or she is wrong.

// If you're an organizer, you might feel very uncomfortable when you're in an ambiguous situation where the rules aren't quite clear or other people are not following them.

// If you're a philosopher, you might get flustered with other people's illogical ideas or "touchy-feely stuff" that feels unnecessary.

// If you're an explorer, you may get really stressed when rules or structure prevent you from checking out new things and doing them your way.

Many times when you run into conflict with someone who "doesn't get it", that person may just be exhibiting her natural preferences, which differ from yours. For example, a person who criticizes your brilliant idea may not mean to discourage you; he could just be expressing his natural inclination toward practicality. Similarly, someone who seems quiet might not be unenthusiastic; he/she could just be thinking deeply before responding.

Knowing how your personality differs from others' enables you to appreciate the unique gifts you and your teammates can offer.

Self-knowledge also helps you position yourself for success in new environments. For example, if you're a Harmonizer, you should probably avoid a job where you have to constantly tell people that they are wrong.

Strengths

Do you ever think, "I wish I could be more _____like that person"? Or "Geez, I hope I'm never _____ like that"? When you're having such thoughts, you're thinking in the language of strengths or weaknesses. Everyone, even the President of the United States, has both strengths and weaknesses. And most people wish they had more strengths and fewer weaknesses.

Some strengths don't really matter much; others shape you profoundly. You may wish you could be more stylish, more buff, or more pimple-free. While those strengths would be fun to have long-term, you'll get further by focusing on building the strengths that make up your character. Imagine what would happen if you lived every day jam-packed with:

Ambition: The determination to reach your goals.

Perseverance: The commitment to overcome obstacles and the temporary "I don't feel like it" sensation.

Courage: The ability to push past your fear to do the right thing.

Assertiveness: Stepping up to respectfully say what needs to be said.

Humor: Making life enjoyable for yourself and others by finding the funny parts.

Orderliness: Keeping your plans, commitments, and belongings in order.

Trustworthiness: Being dependable when it comes to fulfilling important responsibilities and maintaining people's confidence in you.

Kindness: Treating everyone with courtesy and respect.

Enthusiasm: Doing everything with a sense of energy and excitement.

Wow! If you lived every day like that, you'd be able to achieve just about any dream.

But with strengths, more isn't always better. It's possible to have too much of a good thing. For example, if you have too much enthusiasm, other folks may think, "Wow, that guy is such a fake," and be less inclined to work with you. This is true of many strengths. In fact, Aristotle and other ancient philosophers introduced the notion of the Golden Mean. The Golden Mean is kind of like the story of Goldilocks and the Three Bears. That is, the sweet spot often falls right between having too much or too little. Check out the table below to see how this works.

Strength	Too Little	Just Right	Too Much
Ambitious	Lazy	Diligent	Workaholic
Persevering	Quitter	Tough	Stubborn
Courageous	Cowardly	Confident	Cocky
Assertive	Timid	Diplomatic	Combative
Humorous	Stuffy	Friendly	Disrespectful
Orderly	Sloppy	Tidy	Perfectionist
Trustworthy	Flaky	Reliable	Meddlesome
Kind	Selfish	Generous	Martyr
Enthusiastic	"Whatever"	Passionate	Fake

Now that you understand how strengths can vary, use the exercise below to determine your relative strengths.

// Activity //

Take nine sheets of paper. On each one, write down one strength from the list above in big letters (e.g. ambition, perseverance). Flipping through the papers, ask yourself questions such as:

// Which ones seem to come easily or naturally to me?
// Which ones don't come so easily or naturally to me?
// Which ones do I receive compliments and praise about from my teachers, friends, and family?
// Which ones do I receive criticism about from people I trust?

Now, divide your nine sheets of paper into three piles. In the left pile, stack the three sheets that represent your top three strengths. In the right pile, stack the three sheets you believe represent your relative weaknesses. In the middle pile, stack the remaining three sheets of paper. Record in a notebook or

awareness
power

a journal which three you placed in each stack. Now, ask some people who know you really well—your BFFs and family—to do the same exercise, thinking about your strengths and weaknesses. How do they compare? Are there any strengths that you are proud of? Any weaknesses you'd like to improve?

With the list of strengths above, there are "good" and "bad" qualities a person can have. Being a slob or a flake is bad any way you look at it. Personality, however, is different from strengths in this way. There are no right or wrong personalities. Personality is more about how you instinctually prefer to view and interact with the world. Some people prefer big parties while others are more energized by chatting with just a few close friends.

Applying Talent

Given your new knowledge of Talent, its parts — personality and strengths, look at the following questions and reflect on the answers. Use your responses to bolster your understanding of these concepts and learn a bit more about yourself and the people around you.

// Were there any surprises in how you ranked your
     strengths as compared to how others ranked them?
// Can you name someone you know who best characterizes
     each strength?
// Think about someone who's totally different from you?
     How does that affect how you interact and communicate?
// Which of your friends is a strong Harmonizer? Organizer?
     Philosopher? Explorer?

// ALLOCATION

Imagine you are at a train station. You have six dollars in your pocket and the train home costs five dollars. But then you walk by a vending machine and you see a King-Size Snickers. You're really hungry, so you go ahead and buy the Snickers for two dollars. And boy does that Snickers taste good! But then you realize something – you only have four dollars left. And the train costs five dollars.

Because you didn't spend your money on what was important – getting home – and instead spent it on what seemed urgent but wasn't important – the Snickers – you now have an emergency. You have to beg for money from a stranger. Or you have to walk home in the dark. Or you have to call your friend or mom and ask for help.

This train station scenario is a great way to think about life. You have limited time, money, and energy during your life journey. If you spend these precious resources wisely, you can go where you want; if you don't, you'll be stuck.

Allocation is your ability to spend your time, money, and energy wisely. One easy way to allocate things is to split everything you do into one of two categories: the Instant Zone and the Lasting Zone.

Instant Zone: These are all the things in life that don't matter much because they don't help you accomplish your most important goals. Many of the things in the Instant Zone are tempting, like the Snickers Bar. They taste good in the short run, but often leave you unsatisfied.

Lasting Zone: These are all the things in life that do matter, such as getting home on the train. You may be hungry because you didn't eat the Snickers, but you're getting what you really wanted – a ride home.

If you check Facebook for the 47th time in one night, or you send a text message at 3 AM, or you eat your fourth bag of Flaming Hot Cheetos in a day, you're in the Instant Zone.

When you work out, or study ahead of time for a big test, or help your mom with the dishes, you're in the Lasting Zone. You benefit from having a stronger body, doing better in school, and building your relationship with your mother.

Life is an endless tug of war between the Instant Zone and Lasting Zone. Some people have no idea that they are in this tug of war – that every day, every moment, they choose which zone they are in. Successful people understand the value of the Lasting Zone and they allocate their time, energy, and money to things that matter.

Money, Time, and Health

To get a better sense of how the Instant Zone and Lasting Zone differ, consider the chart below. The chart shows different ways that people spend their money, take care of their health, and use their time. What will happen to the person who lives in the Instant Zone? How about the Lasting Zone?

	Instant Zone	Lasting Zone

Money	// Buy latest clothes & gadgets
	// Purchase things they don't
	    need or like
	// Overspending
		// Helping others
		// Saving money
		// Buying essentials
		// Starting a business

Health	// Eating chips & candy
	// Drinking soda
	// Sleeping all day
	// Eating fried foods
		// Working out
		// Eating vegetables
		// Getting regular sleep
		// Drinking lots of water

Time	// Checking Facebook
	// Watching TV
	// Staying up all night
	// Socializing too much
		// Studying
		// Volunteering
		// Working
		// Balancing social time

The person who stays in the Instant Zone will quickly run out of money; or even worse, not know how to manage his/her money as an adult. She will put herself at great risk for diseases like diabetes because she eats junk food and does not work out. It's like there is a hole at the bottom of the Instant Zone column; allocate your money or time here, and like magic, they're gone.

It's the opposite in the Lasting Zone. This person will have a much higher chance of staying healthy, having money to spend on important things, and getting into college or finding a good job. When you allocate your resources into the Lasting Zone, instead of throwing them down the drain, you get something back. You're building toward the future.

awareness
power

But don't think you have to be in the Lasting Zone all the time; that's impossible. Everyone needs some time to relax, watch a little TV, or spend money on something enjoyable.

But you should be in the Lasting Zone much of the time. And it won't be easy, because there are many temptations in the Instant Zone.

There are two easy ways to stay in the Lasting Zone. First of all, stop yourself throughout the day and ask yourself what zone you're in. For example, if you have a choice to eat a vegetable, or a bag of Cheetos, tell yourself, "I'm going to go in the Lasting Zone right now by eating that vegetable." If you've been watching TV for three hours, tell yourself that it's time to move to the Lasting Zone by doing something that makes you better long-term. Develop awareness of what Zone you are in throughout the day and make adjustments.

The other way to stay in the Lasting Zone is to plan your week ahead of time and schedule Lasting Zone activities to make sure you get them done.

Allocating Your Time
Let's use what we know about the Instant Zone and the Lasting Zone to figure out how to allocate one of your most important resources: time.

All of us have exactly 24 hours in a day, 7 days in a week, and 52 weeks in a year. No matter how rich, beautiful, or smart someone is, he/she gets the same 168 hours in a week. The key to using your time well is to identify the difference between the Instant Zone and Lasting Zone.

Remember:

Lasting Zone: Things that matter, usually help you in the long run. Instant Zone: Things that don't matter much, even if they feel good now.

To figure out what matters, start by writing your goals. When you're writing your goals, be sure to include the following:

// **Character:** Describe the kind of character you want to have. For example, you can write, "I want to be hardworking, funny, and respectful."

// **Future:** Describe some things you want to achieve in the future. For example, you might say, "I want to own my own business someday, graduate from college, and travel the world."

// **Now:** Describe the goals you have for life now, both academically and personally. Be sure to list the exact grades you want, how you want to do in activities, and anything else that is important to you.

// **People:** Describe the people in your life who are important. For example, your mother, father, siblings, and boyfriend.

Your goals tell you what matters. To stay in the Lasting Zone, all you have to do is look at your goals and plan things during the week that help you accomplish your goals.

Here's how you do that:

1// **Review your goals:** At the beginning of the week, set aside half an hour to review your goals.

2// **List your weekly action items:** Look at your goals and list all the things you need to do that week to accomplish your goals. These are automatically Lasting Zone activities because they will help you reach your goals.

3// **Put your Lasting Zone action items in your calendar:** Take the list of activities you created and schedule them in your weekly calendar.

4// **Follow your schedule:** Now all you have to do is follow your schedule, and you will automatically be spending lots of time in the Lasting Zone. You can use Google Calendar or other free web-based tools to sync up your schedule with your cell phone.

Stay in the Lasting Zone

Do you know people who always have emergencies? It's always, "Help! I need a ride to the post office before it closes!" Or, "Help! I didn't study for my test, and now I have to cram really quickly!" Or even, "Help! I forget to pack my jersey for the game, and now I need someone to solve my problem!" No matter the situation, there is always a sense of panic and urgency.

Are you getting stressed out just reading about these crises? Fortunately, you can avoid most of this stress and accomplish much more by keeping yourself in the Lasting Zone. When you stay in the Lasting Zone, emergencies are less common because you've planned things out. Here are some ways you can reduce emergencies in your life:

1// **Follow your Weekly Schedule**

Only in cases of real distress — like your house is on fire — should you not do the Lasting Zone activities in your weekly plan. In the train example discussed earlier, this would mean buying the $5 train ticket first, rather than spending your $2 on a Snickers bar. In your everyday life, this means doing your homework, working out, volunteering, practicing, instead of hanging out late at night or responding to the next text message right away.

2// **Create Routines**

It can be hard to remember all the Lasting Zone activities you want to do, so create routines. For example, join a sport or club that meets every day. Or do your homework every day before you watch TV. Or decide to work out every Tuesday, Thursday, and Saturday no matter what. These are automatic Lasting Zone activities that become a part of your life because you made them routine. That's the beauty of a routine; you don't have to think about it — you just do it!

3// **Leave Extra Time**

Make sure you leave some time for Instant Zone activities, or you will burn out. You will also need some extra time in case emergencies come up — even with the best planning, you cannot control everything.

4// **Take Procrastination by the Horns**

A key reason people do not spend time in the Lasting Zone is that it's much easier to procrastinate. It's easier to do the unpleasant things later. When you feel yourself starting to procrastinate, do the following: make a list of all the negative things

31

awareness
power

that will happen if you don't get going immediately. Then make a list of all the positive things that will happen if you finish ahead of time. For example, let's say you need to write a paper. On the positive side you can think about how good it will be to finish early, proofread the paper at your leisure, tell your mom what you did, and hopefully, get a better grade. On the negative side, you might consider how a late start stresses you out and prevents you finishing or what might happen if your printer or Internet connection malfunctions at the last minute. If you convince yourself that you have to get going now because good things will happen (and you will avoid bad things), you can smash the procrastination barrier and complete things before they become emergencies.

// Activity // Which Zone are you in?

Describe some things that you are currently doing in each of the Zones.

	Description of Activity	Time Spent Each Week
Instant Zone		
Lasting Zone		

Are you surprised by how you are allocating your time? What are you observing?

Are there any things you need to eliminate from the Instant Zone?

Applying Allocation

Now that you understand the benefits of staying in the Lasting
Zone and know how to plan your time to do so, look at the following questions and reflect on the answers. Use your responses
to figure out how to spend even more time in the Lasting Zone.

// What are my biggest time wasters?
How can I reduce them?
// What's one important thing I've been putting off?
// What sorts of activities totally energize you?
Where can they be scheduled to keep that energy going?
// What sorts of activities completely drain you? How can
they be scheduled so you can maintain a strong, steady
work flow?

// FOCUS

Imagine you're on YouTube when suddenly, random videos start loading. A baseball game pops up; then a boring classroom lecture; then a red-headed kid playing his guitar. Some videos are in English, but others are in languages you've never heard.

You click on the search bar and refresh the page, but the same thing happens again. You've lost control of your web browser.

This "web-browser-gone-wild" scenario is actually a good way to think about your brain. Like a browser, your mind is always leaping from thought to thought, playing different images, conversations, and videos. One moment you might think about what you want to eat; the next you're focused on your boyfriend or the workout you have to do.

Here's the important question: do you live on auto-pilot, letting your brain roam randomly? Or do you exert control over the videos and programs running on your brain's computer?

For example, imagine that there's a kid who's made fun of you since second grade. Whenever you run into this kid, you see a video in your head in which you're scared and nervous. You instinctively move to the side, letting the kid pass. You hold your breath, hoping he won't see you.

If you knew that your mind was playing a video, just like a browser, couldn't you choose to run a different video? Couldn't you choose to hold your head up, walk straight, and saunter past your tormentor like you owned the world? You could. But only if you're aware of what's happening in your head and have the courage to fight it.

What you think about is called your Focus. You can become a mental ninja by learning to guide your Focus and choosing to pay attention to the things YOU want to pay attention to, rather than letting the world control the videos and programs that run on your mind's browser.

But it won't be easy. Your Focus is so powerful and valuable that everyone wants it; your teachers want it; your girlfriend or boyfriend wants it; advertisers want it; and your parents certainly want it. Maintaining your Focus requires you to check in with yourself each day, and continuously ask, "What am I am thinking about right now and why?"

To see how valuable Focus is, consider this: in the Super Bowl, companies spend three million dollars for one 30-second commercial. That's over $100,000 per second!

And they're happy to pay, because they get something back in return: your mind. These companies know that unless you think about them, you won't buy their product. That's why they're willing to willing to pay big bucks to have their videos play in your head, even if each video only lasts 30 seconds.

How Advertisers Program Your Mind
The world's #1 graduate program in marketing is Northwestern University, where students pay $160,000 for a two-year Master's

35

degree. Here's what marketing students at Northwestern learn about the human mind in the introductory advertising class:

// A human brain is like a warehouse with two types of shelves.

// The first type of shelf is short-term memory. There's not much space in the short-term memory, and whatever is placed here will probably be replaced quickly.

// The second shelf is long-term memory. There is lots of space here; the brain can organize information well; and something put here is likely to remain.

// The advertiser's dream is to place his product on the brain's long-term shelf.

To get any product or idea on the long-term shelf, advertisers do two things:

1// **Frequency:** Play an advertisement constantly.

2// **Variety:** Play an advertisement in different ways. Have you noticed this with Nike? Nike is one of the most well-known companies in the world, but do they ever stop advertising? No. Every year Nike keeps advertising to you because if it doesn't, Nike will get kicked off the long-term shelf, go into your short-term memory, and be forgotten.

And of course, Nike advertises in a variety of ways. They hire famous athletes like LeBron James; they sponsor sporting events; they run TV commercials; they have print advertising. Sometimes they use humor to convince you. Other times they make you feel like a super athlete who can accomplish anything.

And it works, right? Most people know Nike.

What if you did the same thing that Nike and other corporations do? What if you programmed your own mind by continually focusing on images, ideals, goals, and dreams that are important to you? You can. All you have to do is decide what kind of messages you want to give yourself, and then give yourself those messages: 1) frequently 2) in a variety of ways.

For example, if you have a dream of going to college, you can do any of the following:

1// Put up some banners or posters of colleges you would like to attend in your room.
2// Keep a notebook where you record the names of any colleges you would like to learn more about.
3// Watch YouTube videos about the colleges you'd like to attend.
4// Visit college campuses and take notes on what you like and don't like.

What are you doing? You're placing college in the long-term shelving in your brain; you're programming your mind to view yourself as a college student. And you're doing it in a variety of ways. Inevitably, graduating from college will become a part of how you naturally think and act.

Professional athletes do this all the time. A professional golfer will spend hours by him/herself, imagining a golf course in every detail. She will make and play a video in which she hits the

awareness
power

perfect shot at every hole. She will play this video again and again. And then when she is actually golfing, she is able to control her focus. Instead of thinking nervous thoughts, she will think calm, successful ones because she's already programmed her mind to do so.

Now that you know how advertisers get into your head, you should be better prepared to defend your mind and use their techniques to your advantage. Companies hire smart people and give them lots of data, billion-dollar budgets, and one goal: get into the customer's long-term mental warehouse. It's up to you to become a vigilant and strong gatekeeper for your mind and to learn how to focus your brain on what is important to YOU.

Pick Three Movies

Pick three movies or advertisements you want to play in your head over time. These movies could be about succeeding in sports, graduating from high school and college, helping your parents, changing the world, or anything that inspires you. Describe these movies below.

1//
2//
3//

Now, make a plan for how you can keep playing them in your head again and again until they become a part of your long-term mental shelving.

The Power of Questions

One simple way to guide your mind is to control the questions you ask yourself.

For example, if you ask yourself, "In what ways am I blessed?" your mind will automatically think of things such as living in a free country, getting an education, and having friends.

To get yourself depressed all you have to do is ask negative questions. For example, if you ask yourself, "What's wrong with my life?" you will start to play depressing videos in your head. You'll get answers like: "My parents don't give me enough freedom; Maddie is talking about me again; I hate my school."

Don't think you always have to be in "Happy-Happy Land". It's normal to feel sad or dejected sometimes. The point is that by asking good questions, you can control your Focus.

// Activity // Morning Focus Questions

In a CNN interview, the musician Lady Gaga said she starts her day by asking her staff, "How are we going to be brilliant and amazing today?"

Imagine if you woke up every morning and asked yourself, "How can I make today a brilliant day? Is there anyone I can help today? Why am I blessed?" Won't you have a stronger Focus than if you wake up and ask, "Do I really have to get up now?"

Go ahead and pick three powerful, inspiring questions you can ask yourself every morning. Write these questions below, and practice using them this week. Write down the answers you give and how they make you feel.

Morning Questions

1 //
2 //
3 //

Another way to think about your morning questions is to think about the home page on your browser. Your browser's home page opens up automatically every time you jump on the Internet. Because you see your home page all the time, it influences your whole Internet experience. That's what your Morning Questions are like; they are the home page for your mind. They influence and shape your entire life, because you see them every morning. Of course, if you don't have Morning Questions or some other method to focus your mind, you leave your Focus up to the rest of the world — whatever's on the news, or random chance.

Beyond the morning questions, you can also train yourself to ask powerful questions before every debate team competition, basketball practice, or any other recurring activity. Pick questions that help you keep your eyes on the prize, inspire you, and build you up. Ask questions like:

// What can I do today in practice that will seriously improve my game?
// How can I have fun during today's practice?
// What am I excited about today?
// What's great about this situation?
(*Hint: There's always something*).

// How can I turn things around?
// What gives me energy? What drains it?
   How can I do more of what energizes me?
// What's the most important thing that needs to
   happen today?

Before long, you will see the power of controlling your focus through questions.

Mental Blind Spots

When Katie was eighteen, she went to college and made lots of friends. In fact, she made so many friends, that she was one of the most popular people in her college.

But during her second year, something strange happened. Two of her friends sat her down and told her that they thought she was a hard person to be friends with. They told her that whenever they tried to get closer to her, she pushed them away.

Bewildered and a bit hurt, Katie couldn't understand what they were talking about. She knew she wanted close friends…

And then it clicked. When Katie was 16, her sister and best friend, Marcie, died in a car accident. Losing Marcie devastated Katie. Years later, Katie was pushing away all her new friends, and preventing them from becoming close to her, because she was afraid of experiencing pain and sadness if things went wrong.

Like Katie, you have a conscious mind that tells you things such as, "I want friends." You also have an unconscious mind that

41

operates on autopilot. Your unconscious mind's main goal is to protect you from experiencing pain. It may be telling you the opposite of what your conscious mind is telling you, "Don't get too close to friends."

When your unconscious mind is working against your conscious mind, you have what is called a blind spot. **You think you know what you are doing, but really, you have no idea what you are doing.**

The highest level of mental awareness is training yourself to see your blind spots. If you cannot see your blind spots, you'll do the same thing again and again, experience the same pain, and not know what is going on.

The best way to see blind spots is to:

1// **Understand that you have blind spots.** If you think you already know everything about yourself, then you definitely will not see your blind spots. But if you view yourself as a never-ending jigsaw puzzle, your level of self-understanding will continuously improve.

2// **Get others to help you.** Other people can often see things you cannot. Make sure you pay attention to what your friends and loved ones tell you, particularly if you are hearing the same thing from many different people.

3// **Notice Results.** If you keep feeling bad about something, or you keep struggling with something, you may want to think about the reason. Maybe there's something you're not seeing. Maybe you need to talk to someone about it.

Blind spots can also hide positive things. For example, you might not see that you have a talent or skill in a particular area. But once you see your talent, you can develop it.

Applying Focus

Focus doesn't mean you know all your blind spots, have complete control of your mental warehouse, or ask good questions 24x7, just like that. The key take-away is that your mind is a computer that you can train yourself to run, instead of having the outside world run it for you.

Pay attention to what you are thinking about and check in with yourself several times each day. Ask question such as:
// What's going in my mental warehouse right now?
// What questions are running through my head?
// What are my blind spots?

Awareness Power Summary

Your Awareness Power consists of three things:
// Talents: your Strengths and Personality.
// Allocation: your ability to stay in the Lasting Zone.
// Focus: your ability to direct your own mind.

If you have low Awareness Power, you will have no idea how to use your Talents; you will waste precious resources such as time; and others will control your mind easily.

If you have high Awareness Power, you can pick opportunities that match your talents; use your resources to create lasting opportunity; and actively shape your own thinking.

Chapter Two
Social Power

Twenty-five years ago, if two people wanted to stay in touch, they could:

// Drive or fly to see each other in person
// Write a letter
// Talk on a phone wired to the wall
// Send a fax

That was it.
Today, friends can connect in those four ways and more:

// Email
// Instant message
// Cell phone
// Text message
// Facebook
// Twitter
// Video chat
// Online photo albums
// Blogs

Connecting to others has never been easier. You can talk to your friends via cell phones and the Internet. You can take photos and share them instantly. You can connect with people around the globe whom you've never met — and as a bonus, Google will even translate your words into another language for free.

So the question is not, "Can you connect?" The question is, "Can you do anything with your connections?" If you can use your connections to make the world better, help someone who desperately needs it, or help yourself, then you have incredible power.

Your ability to help yourself and others through your social connections is called your Social Power. People with high Social Power can find new jobs faster, meet boyfriends and girlfriends more easily, and gain access to many interesting social opportunities.

But increasing your Social Power takes much more than having lots of Facebook friends. It requires serious commitment, strategy, and a sincere desire to help others.

You can increase your Social Power by focusing on three key areas: **Network, Service, and Diversity.**

// NETWORK

Imagine there weren't any paved roads in the United States. No highways. No asphalt-coated local roads. Just uneven dirt and gravel roads.

How much longer would it take to get around? The four-hour drive from Miami to Orlando might take days. Driving across the country could take months.

Fortunately, we do have a system of highways that connects all our major cities. Built in the 1950's, our road network makes it possible for all of us to travel more easily and safely.

Just like there is a network of roads that connects cities smooth-ly, there are networks of friends that connect people. If you have strong connections to lots of people, you can get what you want more easily, quickly, and safely.

For example, imagine that you're going to the movies and there is a long line. You're worried about missing the first five minutes, and you probably won't have time to buy popcorn.

But then your neighbor, who owns the theatre, sees you. Because he knows you, he moves you up to the front, gets you a free drink, and won't mind if you stick around to watch several more movies for free. Everything got easier and faster because he's a part of your network. While that may seem unfair to the other people waiting in line, it doesn't change this fact: *things are generally easier when you know people.*

Your network is made of the people you know. The more people you know, the stronger your network. The better your relationship with each of those people, the stronger your network.

For example, if the person at the theatre had been someone at school who knew you, but didn't like you, you might have found yourself waiting longer than everybody else. And while that also might seem unfair, that's the world we live in.

If you develop a strong network, you will get better jobs, meet more interesting people, get what you want faster, and hold greater power and ability to help everyone else in your network.

Think Backwards

To get what you want, you sometimes have to do the opposite of what you want. For example, think about what it takes to steer a rowboat if you're sitting at the front. To go right, you have to paddle on your left side. To go left, you have to paddle on your right side.

Building a strong social network is similar. If you want everyone else to help you, you have to first help everyone else. If you want people to give you the hook up, you have to first hook up other people.

For example, imagine that you've won a $1,000 scholarship from a group of businesspeople in your town. The businesspeople throw a breakfast in your honor, and you find yourself seated at a table of fifty-year-olds.

They start asking you questions about what sports you play and what you like to do in your free time. You respond to everything, but after a while they stop asking new questions. The conversation dies down, and you start to think, "Wow, this is going to be a long breakfast. These people are so boring."

You find the businesspeople boring because they didn't bring up enough things that interested you. But what if the businesspeople find you boring because you didn't bring up any topics that interested them? You didn't ask them about their businesses, their families, what their lives were like when they were in high school, their dreams, or why they wanted to give away $1,000 in the first place.

We want other people to be interested in us, our dreams, and our goals. We want others to help us. *But the master social networkers do the opposite.* They spend their time asking other people questions, helping other people accomplish their goals, and expressing an interest in others.

So if you want others to…
//   Help you, help others first.
//   Talk to you, talk to them first.
//   Be interested in you, be interested in them first.

It won't always work. Sometimes you'll help others or express an interest in them and you won't get anything in return. That's okay. Everything you do should be real and genuine anyway, and if it is, in the long run, you will have a strong, powerful network.

// **Activity** // Think Backwards

1// Write down the names of three people you know well. These people could be your family members or friends.

2// For each person, describe three things you think they want or need.

3// For each person, find one thing you can do to help them get what they want or need.

When you start by helping others, they value you and are more likely to help you when you need it.

How to Network

As human beings, we are naturally wired to think about our own lives — what we will eat, wear, drink, and do. But the golden rule of networking is to be outwardly-focused. If you take an interest in what others are doing—what they need and how you can help them, they will be interested in you.

Here are four simple ways to build your network. You can use these methods now, in college, and when you're an adult.

1// **Join groups and organizations.**

Join groups you enjoy such as a sports team or community theatre, or volunteer somewhere, an animal shelter for example. When you're joining these groups, you'll naturally meet people without having to worry about networking. You'll meet friends, coaches, and advisors who you will get to know through practices, games, and events. As long as you've been a good buddy, colleague, or teammate, you'll get support when you need it. In contrast, if you just

49

social
power

go home and sit by yourself, you'll miss opportunities to connect with great people.

2// **Balance quality and quantity.**

If you find yourself in a room filled with one hundred people for two hours, it's smarter to have really strong conversations with four or five people who will remember you than it is to run around and shake everyone's hand. Anyone can get 5000 friends on Facebook if they invite everyone he encounters, regardless of whether there is a real connection or not. But a network's strength depends on its quality as well as its quantity. So aim for a balance: connect with lots of interesting people, but make sure you have a home base of strong friendships.

3// **Seek out mentors.**

A mentor is someone who can provide advice, introduce you to people who can help you, or provide an outside perspective. Mentors are often older than you are, but that is not always the case. For example, if you plan to join the military, someone who is currently in the military would be a great mentor.

Here are some ways to connect with mentors:

// **Develop a positive reputation.** Mentors naturally want to find young people who are hard workers and respectful, so they will seek you out.

// **Ask adults in your life if they can mentor you.** You can look for mentors at your religious organization or another group you belong to, or through your parents' friends. It's okay to ask someone to mentor you directly. You could say, "I really value your perspective and know I would benefit from your wisdom and experience. Would you be willing to mentor me? If you're busy, we could have just a couple of phone calls a year."

// **Set up appointments.** Whenever you meet an adult you find interesting, ask that person if you can call him or meet with him for half an hour to learn more about how they got to where they are. If the conversation goes well, you can ask them to mentor you. Many people want to help young people, so don't be shy in seeking out mentors.

// **Establish Timing:** You should ask your mentor how often he or she would like to talk. For example, some people speak with a mentor once every 6 months, and others check in with a mentor every week.

You will always benefit from having mentors, even when you reach adulthood.

And of course, just like you want older people to mentor you, you should mentor younger people. Volunteer in your elementary school, your place of worship, or your neighborhood. Besides being the right thing to do, you are telling the world, "I get it. If I expect people to help me, I also have to be willing to help other people."

How NOT to Network

There are a couple of major no-no's that can kill your networking game.

1// **Calling others only when you need them.**

You know that person who only calls you when she needs $20? Or when her car is in a ditch, and she needs you to push it out? Or that guy who forgets you exist until his girlfriend dumps him, and he need friends again? How do you react when those people call you? You're probably thinking, "The only time you ever call me is when you need something!"

To avoid falling into this category, call others when you don't need them. Call a friend to see how the big event went, or just to say hi, or to wish her a happy birthday. And yes, if you're dating someone, make sure you still make time for your friends, or they might not make time for you when you need them. The best time to build a bridge is before you need to cross it.

2// **Keeping score.**

Don't call someone up and say, "Listen, I helped you with your homework that one time in March, and I also listened to you ramble for hours about your girlfriend last week. Now, I need someone to clean my basement, and I expect some repayment."

Not only will people think you're crazy and but they'll also feel like you were helping them because you expected something in return. The best way to network is to assume that what goes around comes around. Don't expect anything from anyone. Just trust that when you're there for people, they'll probably want to be there for you too.

In all walks of life, there are always a few folks who just take, take, take and never give. It will become pretty obvious to you who those people are, and you can choose to limit your interactions with them in the future. Just be sure you're not That Guy or Gal.

3// **Manipulating others.**

Can you tell when someone is talking to you just because he or she wants to get something from you? As human beings, we have a 6th sense that lets us know when people are faking. The best way to network is to be real. Be interested in others because you are interested in others; help others because you want to help others. If you can't find a way to connect genuinely with someone, then maybe that person shouldn't be a part of your network.

Applying your Network

Now that you know the right way to build your network, look at the following questions and reflect on the answers.

// Who are the top five most influential people in my life?
// What can I do for them to help let them know I value and appreciate them?
// Who would be an outstanding mentor for me?

// SERVICE

At age 18, Janelle moved from Frankfort, Kentucky to Miami, Florida. Miami was so much bigger than Frankfort! The lights seemed brighter, the trees greener, the people happier, the weather noticeably warmer.

But then reality hit. Janelle had left behind everything. All of her friends were someplace else. And her job stunk; she had to make painful phone calls all day long selling fireplace accessories.

Janelle moped around, wrote depressing poems, and cried on her drive to work. One day she called her best friend from back home to complain. In a state of frustration, her friend said, "Janelle, you're the most miserable person I know."

Her friend's harsh words jarred Janelle. So Janelle gave herself a new mission — to help others in any way she could. She figured, "I already feel miserable. I might as well try to improve someone else's life."

First, Janelle called a girl she knew was going through a tough time. She invited her to coffee, and listened to her talk about her problems for an hour. Janelle listened without expecting anything in return.

When a married couple Janelle had only met once mentioned they were going out of town for three weeks, Janelle offered to check on their place and pick up their mail while they were gone. When another person was going out of town, Janelle gave her a ride to the airport.

Janelle dogsat. She babysat. She volunteered at a non-profit.

Eight months later, Janelle's life looked completely different. She was surrounded by friends who cared about her and called her often. And she had a new job. The non-profit Janelle had volunteered at appreciated Janelle so much that they hired her! No more phone calls selling fake fire logs!

Janelle's story illustrates a powerful truth: when we serve others, we increase our value to them. People want to befriend us, hire us, and connect with us because we make their lives better.

Every single hero, whether real, like Dr. Martin Luther King, Jr. or imaginary, like Spiderman, is a hero because he helped others. Heroes make the world better and that's why the world admires them. If you want to be heroic, all you have to do is make the world better.

Service can be small, like helping a kid cross the street, or big, like spending the whole summer volunteering. It can be hard work, like getting on your knees to clean an elderly neighbor's basement, or fun, like playing in a charity 3-on-3 basketball tournament. Regardless of how you do it, there is no more powerful way to build your Social Power than to serve.

How to Serve

It's not always easy to know how to serve, so here are five ways you can get started today:

1// Start with what's around you.

Serving doesn't have to be complicated. A lot of the time it's just a matter of volunteering to help with the task at hand. If you know your mom has had a long day at work and is stressed about the messy house, take the initiative to help clean up without being asked. Stay after a school assembly to help fold up chairs, or help someone carry boxes to their car.

2// Meet emotional needs.

You can serve others by caring about what they're going through. If someone you know has been sick, has recently lost a loved one, or is just going through a rough time, you can offer encouragement by sending them a card or paying them a visit. Even though you can't change these circumstances for them, letting them know they're not alone during hard times can provide encouragement.

3// Use your talents and skills.

Look for ways to serve that use your talents. If you're a good cook, make some cookies. If you're a pro at landscaping, offer to mow someone's lawn. Spiderman used his web slinging talents to serve others and become a superhero. When you use your talents to serve others, you become a real-life superhero.

However, always serve with an eye toward others' needs. You wouldn't want to make cookies for a diabetic who can't eat them or offer to mow the lawn of someone who lives in a mobile home.

4// **Keep your commitments.**

If you volunteer to serve at a soup kitchen or help out at an animal shelter, it can feel like real work. And about the time you're supposed to show up for your volunteer duties, you might prefer to go to the movies with your friends. But if you don't keep your commitments, you're actually hurting, rather than helping. As a result, be sure to only commit to things you can do, and follow through on your commitments.

5// **Let others serve you.**

You know that warm fuzzy feeling you get when you give someone a gift you know he or she will really like? Every time you let someone serve you in a special way, you allow him or her to know the blessing of giving. Part of being a good friend is also allowing others to be a friend to you. Be sure to let others know how they can help and support you.

Fight for Dignity

John's dad and mom both lost their jobs and their family is barely scraping by. Christmas is approaching, and there's no way his parents can get John a present.

You talk to John's parents and offer to give John a present. You have two choices:

1// You can show up at John's house and present the wrapped gift to him three days before Christmas.

2// You can meet John's parents ahead of time and give them the present to give to him on Christmas morning.

In option 1, you are the hero and you get the satisfaction of helping John.

In option 2, the parents are the heroes, because they give John the present.

Option 2 is stronger because it preserves dignity for John's parents. Instead of saying, "We're so broke that we can't get you anything but we found someone who can," John's parents get to preserve their role as providers and say, "Here's your present, son."

When you serve, you should always try to preserve the dignity of whoever is being served. Dignity is an individual's basic self-worth and self-respect.

If the elderly woman next door needs help cleaning her basement, can you do it in a way that makes her feel special, as if she's doing you the favor? If you want to invite the kid with no friends to your party because you want to include him, can you do it in a way that builds his dignity?

One of the fine lines you will face when you serve is, "How do you help people while preserving their dignity?"

Challenge Yourself to Solve Root Problems
What happens if you cut a few leaves off a weed? The weed comes back, right? If you want to remove the weed, you have to cut out its root.

Service is the same way. You could tie your little brother's shoes every morning for him. Or you could teach him how to tie his own shoes. Teaching him to tie his own shoes will take longer and require more patience, but it solves the root problem: He doesn't know how to tie his shoes.

You won't always be able to do it, but it can be fun to ask yourself: Is there a way for me to solve the real problem here?

For example, let's say your service club wants to clean the local park. You find all sorts of litter and debris everywhere and you clean it. Now, you can take things one step further and ask yourself, "Is there something we can do that would keep this park clean year round?"

Can you solve this problem at its root? Can you get a meeting with the city council or the neighborhood association to discuss long-term solutions? Can you do something that no one else in your town, or state, or country has done?

See the Invisible

When Jack was in first grade, he did not have any friends. He wasn't good at sports; he wore large bifocals; and his classmates generally avoided him. The worst days of the year for Jack were when his classmates had birthdays. Why? Because no one ever invited him to a birthday party, Jack always had to hear his classmates discuss how much fun they had or were going to have.

Toward the end of the year, Mary, one of Jack's classmates, invited him to her birthday. It was a simple act for Mary, but it was something that Jack remembered for the rest of his life. Jack explains it this way, "When I was invisible; when no one saw me; when everyone ignored me, Mary *saw* me."

Seeing those who are invisible, who don't have friends, who aren't the popular kids, is one of the most powerful ways to serve. When you reach out to invisible people— the new kid who's struggling to fit in, the kid who doesn't have friends, the immigrant kid who is just learning English—and do it in a way that preserves their dignity and recognizes their self-worth, you will have massive impact.

There are three ways to distinguish yourself as a leader when it comes to service:

1// Do everything in a manner that honors people's dignity.
2// Solve root problems.
3// See those who are Invisible.

Applying Service
Now that you've learned more about the power of Service, consider the following questions and reflect on the answers.

// Who in your community is invisible? Is there someone that everyone ignores? How can you see and value this person?
// Are there any pressing problems in your community that you can help solve?
// List three things that you are good at or enjoy. Next to each thing, think of how you could use your talent or passion to help others.

// DIVERSITY

Remember the road network analogy? Imagine that Florida had ten highways all of which went from Orlando to Tampa Bay, but to no other cities. It'd be great if you wanted to drive from Orlando to Tampa; there'd be no traffic with all those lanes.

But what if you needed to go to Miami or up to Atlanta? It'd take forever, right?

Your social network is the same way. If you're only friends with football players, all you'll have easy access to is football players. But if you're friends with football players, musicians, and artists, you'll have access to a lot more people.

Your ability to connect to people different from you determines your network's Diversity. If your network is diverse, you have access to all sorts of people — old, young, rich, poor, shy, outgoing, athletic, musical, Black, White, Hispanic, Asian, and Native American.

You'll get invited to different types of parties; you'll eat at different restaurants; you'll learn about different job opportunities. But this will only happen if you know different types of people.

Power of New Environments

Today we know a simple way to add 17 and 14. We can just line up the digits, carry the one, and get 31.

$$
\begin{array}{r}
17 \\
+\,14 \\
\hline
31
\end{array}
$$

But until about 1200 AD, Europe had a different numbering system called Roman numerals. In Roman numerals, 17 is written XVII and 14 is XIV, so our problem from above would look like the figure below:

$$\begin{array}{r} XVII \\ +XIV \\ \hline \end{array}$$

If you can't see an easy way to do this problem, that's because there isn't one. Imagine how hard it would be to multiply, divide, or do fractions and higher level math with large numbers if they were written in Roman numerals. For example, the number 34,498 in Roman numerals is:

MMMMMMMMMMMMMMMMMMMMMMMMMMMMMMMMMMCDXCVIII

How did Europe learn the improved numbering system that we all use today? In about 1200, a young man named Leonardo Fibonacci travelled throughout Northern Africa with his father. Leonardo interacted with people from all over Asia, North Africa and the Middle East.

Some of the people Leonardo met conducted all their business and math using the 1,2,3,4 decimal system we use today. When Leonardo arrived back in Italy, he wrote a famous book called *Book of Calculation* that shared the new numeric system and more.

Book of Calculation was read widely in Europe. Subsequently, the economy in Europe skyrocketed and Italy in particular became the world's business and cultural capital, due in no small part to the improved mathematical system. Artists built great wonders such as the Sistine Chapel; scientists like Galileo made earth-shifting discoveries; and Europe planted the seeds for the technological breakthroughs that we enjoy today.

What was the key to Leonardo's impact? He went to a new environment where he met people who thought and acted differently. One of the best ways to increase your network's diversity is to change your environment. Over the summer, go to a camp and meet new people; work at a different job; join a new school club; volunteer somewhere new. Change your environment so that you have to meet people you would not normally meet.

Even if you don't change world history, you'll change yourself as you encounter new people who teach you new things and introduce you to new opportunities.

Go Beyond Surface Diversity
When Sue was 16 years old, her parents got divorced and Sue's dad moved out. Sue's mother didn't make much money and they barely paid their mortgage every month. Sue missed her father desperately.

Sue had several good friends at school and she was close to her art teacher. But Sue never told anyone about her challenges at home. In fact, her best friend was shocked to find out nine years later, that Sue's parents had been divorced.

Why did Sue not tell anyone? Sue is from Korea. In Korean culture, you are often taught not to share challenges you are having at home with people outside your family. Korea is not the only country to have such a culture. In Ethiopia, there is a saying, "Never reveal the mysteries of your home to the outside world." In other words, keep your mouth shut!

In U.S. culture, openness is generally considered a good thing. Many students would tell their friends about problems at home and maybe even ask people at their places of worship to pray for them as they struggled with a challenge.

But Sue's story shows why things we can see on the outside – like race and gender – don't actually tell us very much when compared to things we cannot easily see.

For example, an American might define freedom as "doing what you want" or "pursuing your life dreams". Someone from a developing country where elders and tradition have tremendous power might define freedom as "doing what my elders, culture, and tradition want me to do." You might think an arranged marriage violates freedom, and he or she might think dating violates freedom. Why? Because you have different definitions of freedom.

The point isn't that you have to know the definitions, customs, and beliefs of every culture or person. The point is that surface diversity such as race and gender don't tell us much compared to beliefs and cultures. As you're building a diverse network, train yourself to pay attention to the hidden forces that may drive your interactions.

For example, in the United States, we are used to speaking directly. If I'm trying to do business with your company, I can have a meeting; tell you what I have to offer; ask you if you want it; and get a quick yes or no. Now imagine a country where such direct talk is considered rude and disrespectful. If you present your offer immediately, you will lose the sale. But if you wait until the third or fourth meeting to talk business, you increase your chances of landing the million-dollar contract.

// Activity // Your Definitions

Words like respect, freedom, self-expression, and control can mean wildly different things, depending on where someone is from. For example, small town life is different from life in New York City; norms in a first-world country differ from those in a developing country; and big families operate differently from small families. Since every single culture and every single person is different, it requires skill and practice to quickly decode what's really driving someone's behavior. But before you can understand someone else's culture and beliefs, you have to understand your own, starting with how you define your values.

For each of the words below, write your definition, including anything that comes to mind when you see the word. There are no right or wrong answers. Just write what leaps into your head.

Freedom
Openness
Love
Authority
Respect
Friendship

Now, below your definition for each word write "opposite", and describe the opposite of what you believe.

If you had to work with a person who believed the opposite of what you did, how would you do it?

Take a final look at your definitions. **Are there any that you want to change? What would you change them to?**

Challenges to Creating a Diverse Network

There are many reasons to reach out to people who are different from you.

// Researchers at business schools have shown that those with diverse networks make more money and get better jobs.
// Like Leonardo Fibonacci, you can learn new things that make life much easier.
// It's good to practice now, because you may have to study or work in another country some day.

Despite these many reasons, connecting to diverse peoples is not always easy. Here are a few challenges you may have to overcome.

// Diversity means that you cannot have it your way all the time. If someone is different from you, and you want to have a real connection with him/her, there will be times when you have to watch his/her movie, listen to his/her music, eat his/her food, and talk about what he/she wants

to talk about. Choosing to develop a diverse network
means choosing to give up your way some of the time.
// Creating a diverse network requires tremendous confidence. When you interact with diverse people, those
who are like you may feel like you are ignoring them, and
those who aren't like you may not always welcome you.

But if you have confidence, you can stay strong and carve out
your own path. You can forge friendships and connections
among a diverse group of people, learn new and challenging
ideas, and prepare yourself for success in the global economy.

Applying Diversity
Now that you have had a chance to think more about Diversity,
look at the following questions and reflect on the answers. Use
your responses to figure out how you can connect with people
who are different from you.

// What are some of the key characteristics that make
up your identity (e.g. age, race, gender, interests,
personal traits)?
// What kinds of people do you currently have in
your network?
// Who could you connect with that's different than you?

Social Power Summary
Your Social Power consists of three things:
// Network: The size and strength of your network.
// Service: Your level of contribution to others.
// Diversity: Your connections to a wide range of people.

If you have low Social Power, you will face life's challenges and opportunities alone; you will rarely experience the joy of helping others; and you will confine yourself to people like yourself.

If you have high Social Power, you and your network will create opportunities together; you will leave the world better than you found it; and you will have access to diverse people and ideas.

Chapter Three
Solution Power

Michael Jordan is widely considered the greatest basketball player who's ever lived. Jordan led the league in scoring for ten seasons, won five Most Valuable Player awards, and captured six NBA Championship titles. Jordan's famous "hang time" allowed him to dunk almost at will on anyone, even seven footers.

But none of those things made Jordan the greatest. Jordan's excellence came down to one thing: he consistently found a way to win, even in the most challenging and unwinnable situations. Down by three points with one second to go in a playoff game? No problem. Jordan would bury a three pointer over two people guarding him.

Down by fifteen points in the fourth quarter? No problem. Jordan would steal the ball and block shots on defense, make incredible passes on offense, and of course, add his own shots.

When it counted the most, Jordan somehow found a way.

In life, you will often have to find a way, even if no way seems possible.

When J. K. Rowling tried to publish Harry Potter, she was

rejected more than ten times. **More than ten publishers read Harry Potter and concluded the book would not make money.** For J. K. Rowling, the solution was to keep trying in the face of rejection. Today, of course, J. K. Rowling is the second richest woman in England, behind Queen Elizabeth II, and Harry Potter is among the bestselling series of all time.

Sometimes solving problems won't be a matter of trying harder, but being more creative. For example, one university passed out a book containing everyone's photos and background information to the freshmen class every year. One student pushed himself to create a better system. He gave his classmates a way to post their own pictures and connect with other classmates. And that's how Facebook was started. It wasn't about trying harder – it was about doing something differently.

Your ability to solve problems, whether in sports, school, at home, or at work is called your Solution Power. To build your Solution Power, you will want to increase your **Creativity, Persuasion, and Flexibility.**

// CREATIVITY

William had a problem. He didn't have electricity in his small village in Malawi, East Africa. Because he didn't have electricity, William didn't have lights in his home, and he couldn't listen to his favorite music on the radio.

One day, William went to the village library and found a book called *Using Energy*. The book explained how windmills generate electricity.

William did not have a Home Depot or a hardware store where he could pick up the tools and parts to build a windmill. So he worked with what he had. He built the main structure of the windmill by using wood from a tree that grew near his village. He built the rotator to turn the windmill out of bicycle parts. Piece by piece, he built a windmill.

Before long, William's windmill generated enough electricity to light his home and power a radio! William's story, told in his best-selling book, *The Boy who Harnessed the Wind*, highlights the power of using creativity to solve problems.

Creativity is the ability to think differently and come up with new answers. Without creativity, we would still be riding around in horse-drawn buggies. Or worse, we wouldn't even know how to make wheels.

Everything you see around you is the result of someone's creativity. Someone designed the chair you are sitting in; someone created the machine that wove the material of your clothes;

71

someone created your cell phone, computer, the flooring in your house, and the formula for the concrete that makes up the sidewalk outside your home.

What will you create in life?

If you train yourself to think creatively, like William did, you will solve problems in new and often amazing ways. Seemingly impossible challenges such as a lack of electricity can disappear when you employ creativity.

What if There Were a Way?

There's one question you can ask again and again in order to generate creative solutions to difficult problems. When in doubt ask, "What if there were a way to _____?"

"What if there were a way for man to fly?" This question gave us the airplane.
"What if there were a way to see after the sun set?" This question gave us the light bulb.
"What if there were a way for people to communicate on the go?" This question gave us— you guessed it—the cell phone.

Now try asking these questions about your own life:
// What if there were a way for you to study in another country over the summer? *You can. Start by researching exchange programs.*
// What if there were a way for you to get your dream internship? *You can, if you network aggressively or volunteer to get relevant experience.*

// What if there were a way for you to make more than
$15/hour? How about more than $20/hour?
You can, by starting your own mowing service or another
business of your choosing.

Being open to new ideas is the foundation of creativity. If you say,
"There's no way it will happen," then you've immediately killed
your opportunity to be creative. For example, imagine if William
had said "There is no way for me to have electricity." He wouldn't
have even considered the option of building a windmill.

"Yes, and…"
There is a simple creativity exercise that is often used on
Saturday Night Live, and by many comedians. Here's how it
works: no matter what, you have to agree with whatever the
other person says. You have to say, **"Yes and…"** even if you feel
like saying "No."

For example, if someone comes up to you and says, "I think
you're a jerk," you say, "Yes, and I'm also the world's biggest idiot."

If your teacher tells you, "You're getting better at math," you say,
"Yes, and I think I look like Einstein, too."

In these situations, you could disagree, but if you do, you'll kill the
creativity, not to mention the humor.

Here's what a "Yes, and…" exchange between you and your
friend might like look like:

Your friend: "I don't think you'll ever get a date."
You: "Yes, and that's why I've decided to go live by myself in Antarctica."
Your friend: "Yes, and maybe you should just move to Mars."
You: "Yes, and maybe I'll have to move to my own corner on Mars, because none of the Martians will date me."

Some people would say, "My feelings are hurt. You said I'll never get a date." But by saying "Yes and…," you can create humor, and an original, unpredictable conversation.

In the same way, if you're willing to entertain new ideas or thoughts that are the opposite of what comes naturally, you can create new, unpredictable solutions.

For example, if you're in a brainstorming session, and someone throws out a crazy idea, instead of killing it, build on it. If your mom asks you do to something that you don't like, try to build on it and turn it into something you both like. Don't dismiss new or strange ideas, use your powers of creativity to explore them and see a new perspective.

"Yes, and…" // Activity //

Write out a hypothetical conversation between a friend and yourself.

Choose from one of the following opening lines. Remember, you have to agree with the statement, and keep building on it.

// Your cell phone is a kangaroo.
// You scored three touchdowns in the last Super Bowl.
// Cafeteria food is delicious.

You can also try having an actual conversation with someone to see how it turns out and enjoy the laughs.

Other Creative Methods
There are many methods you can use to become more creative. Here are some of them:

1// Brainstorm
Gather a group of people and share ideas about an important topic. You might ask a question like, "How should we _____?" Write what everyone says on a whiteboard or a piece of chart paper and build on each other's ideas. Consider every contribution, no matter how weird. Good ideas often come from crazy ideas that are tweaked just a little bit.

2// Ask Questions
Ask people lots of questions. A great question is, "Help me understand _____." "Help me understand what it's like to be a teacher, a mom, or a firefighter."

3// Research
You can Google "how to be more creative" and find many logic puzzles and games that challenge your mind, which will ultimately enhance your creativity.

The keys as you learned from William and "Yes, and…" activities are:

// When facing a problem, assume a solution is possible. Ask yourself, "What if there were a way to…"
// It's always easy to dismiss something and disagree. Instead, say "Yes, and…"

Applying Creativity

Now that you have had a chance to think more about Creativity, look at the following questions and reflect on the answers. How could you be more creative in the following week?

// William used the things around him to generate electricity? What can you create using the things you already have?
// What problems do you currently have? List them out and ask yourself what you can do to solve them? If the answer is nothing, push yourself to come up with an answer anyway.
// Is there anyone in your life who teases you? What if you agreed with their teasing and said "Yes and…" Wouldn't it defuse the situation?

// PERSUASION

In 2011, the National Association of College Employers surveyed over 170 employers and asked them what quality they valued most when hiring college graduates. The #1 response was verbal communication.

Why is communication so important? Communication allows you to get support for your ideas. Almost anything important in life requires you to get a "yes" from somebody. If you want…

// A job, you need to convince someone to hire you.
// A boyfriend or girlfriend, you need to convince someone to date you.
// An apartment, you need to convince the landlord you won't trash his/her place.
// To attend college, you need to convince the college to accept you.
// Customers for your business, you need to persuade them to buy what you're selling.

Persuasion is your ability to communicate in a way that gets support for your ideas. You could be the smartest person in the world, but if you can't persuade anyone of anything, you'll be stuck. On the flipside, by mastering a few basics of persuasive communication, you can solve many problems.

How to Convince People of Almost Anything

Persuasive communication is the art of convincing others to support your ideas, whether written or verbal.

To see how persuasive communication works, let's consider something absurd that no one would ever agree to do. Let's pretend you want your city to create a giant, 50-foot statue of you and put it in the middle of the city where everyone can see it. Let's say you live in Orlando, Florida.

You have 15 minutes to convince the City Council and Mayor to build the statue. What will you say?

You had better be prepared because they're going to be thinking, "This kid is not only crazy, but he has the biggest ego of anyone we've ever met. There's no way we're even considering this."

You could try to force them into doing it by yelling, "DO IT BECAUSE I SAID SO!" But that probably won't work. Research has shown that force is a relatively ineffective method of communication. Even if someone does what you want them to do, using force may cause them to resent you, or give a half-hearted effort.

Even in this ridiculous situation, if you understand persuasive communication, you can present a strong case. Here are some techniques you can use to present your case effectively:

1// **Focus on what your audience wants.**
When you are trying to persuade someone to do something, focus on what they want, not what you want. If you want your parents to get you a car, explain how it will save them time because they won't have to pick you up anymore. Explain how it will help you get into college because you can study in places far away from your distracting friends.

78

To get the statue built, don't focus on the statue. Focus on things that a mayor would want, such as increasing tourism in Orlando, keeping the city clean, or inspiring kids to do better in school, and show the mayor how erecting the statue will give him these things.

2// Use numbers that make your point.

Some people only listen to arguments that include data and numbers. As a result, be sure to bolster your case with strong data such as:

// "I conducted a survey with 200 students in Orlando, and 98% of them said it would be inspiring to have a statue of a young person in the center of town."

// "I counted the number of statues in town, and out of 385 statues, only 3 are of kids. That means that less than 1% of this city's statues are of young people, even though we make up 18% of the total population. Clearly, we are underrepresented in this city. What kind of message does it send to young people if we are left out in 99% of our community's statues? It makes us feel like we don't matter."

3// Tell stories that inspire emotion.

Some people are more motivated by emotion than numbers, so it's a good idea to include at least one inspiring story in your presentation. You might explain how another statue inspired someone to do something heroic, and then ask, "What heroic actions will our statue inspire?"

4// Show that others are doing it.

People often feel more comfortable about doing something

if they see others have already done it successfully. Find and share the stories of three other towns that successfully created a statue of a young person.

5// **Borrow credibility.**

Find someone who is respected and show that he or she like your ideas. For example, you can go on Google and find some quotes from a famous city planner or psychologist who supports your argument. You can also find an expert who lives near you and ask him or her to come with you to speak to the City Council.

If you build your argument persuasively, you can communicate the following:

// I can help you accomplish some of your most important goals, such as inspiring youth in Orlando.

// I have data to support what I'm proposing.

// I have some great stories that show what's possible.

// There are other people who have done what I'm suggesting and achieved great results.

// Finally, there are credible experts who believe this type of project is important.

// If you like this idea, I humbly suggest that the statue be in my likeness to inspire other kids to take an idea and bring it to life.

Next time you need something, think about these techniques of persuasion. You can always try to force people, but force is amateurish, relatively ineffective, and often unnecessary. Use the five persuasive communication techniques you've learned as a starting point. There are many more strategies you can find in books and articles, but if you start with the basics, you're likely to make great progress.

1// Focus on what your audience wants.
2// Use numbers that support your point.
3// Tell stories that inspire emotion.
4// Show that other people agree.
5// Borrow credibility.

// Activity // Use Your Powers of Persuasion

How might you use persuasive communication to convince your parents that your curfew should be pushed pack to ten on school nights, instead of nine?

For example, can you find some research that shows that roads are safer after 9:30 because they are less crowded? Can you present supporting evidence by highlighting three instances when you stayed out until ten with special permission, and handled yourself well?

What could you say other than, "I'm older now so I deserve it?"

Verbal Communication:
Four Steps to Giving a Great Speech

Speaking in public has been ranked by many people as more frightening than death. But sometimes, to get support for your ideas, you will have no choice but to speak.

Speaking in public doesn't have to terrify you. If you follow the following four steps, you can be a rock-star presenter.

81

solution
power

1// **Know your audience.**

The speech you'd give to kindergarten students should be very different from the speech you'd give to U.S. Marines. Know your audience! Before you speak, answer the following questions:

// What is the goal of the presentation?

// How long do you have to speak?

// Who exactly will be in the audience? How many people will there be? What are their ages and professions?

By asking a few questions ahead of time, you can figure out your audience and understand how to best meet their needs.

2// **Outline Your Presentation.**

Outline your entire presentation, from start to finish. This means that you should be clear about what your primary message is, and create a plan to present your argument, or point of view, step by step.

In your outline, be sure to include:

// Your introduction and conclusion.

// Short, engaging stories and examples that make your points.

// Evidence that supports your points. Remember the principles of persuasive communication!

// A call to action, or an appeal to the audience to do some-thing new or different as a result of your presentation.

There are many books that will show you how to outline your speeches and presentations in detail. One great book is *Give Your Speech, Change the World* by Nick Morgan.

3// **Rehearse your presentation.**

Once you have your outline, rehearse your presentation with a stopwatch until you are comfortable with it. Do not try to memorize the entire presentation word for word. This rarely works, and will only stress you out as you try to remember exactly what you wanted to say.

One great rehearsal technique is to practice each part — the introduction, each story, and the conclusion, separately. Then, once you've rehearsed each part and know it well, run through the entire speech from beginning to end.

On the day of the presentation, wake up early and rehearse the presentation at least once. Do not skip rehearsal. Even professional athletes do warm-ups and review their game-tapes before a game; you can to do the same.

4// **Speak with Passion.**

The audience needs to connect with you as a person, not just with the content of your speech. When you present, speak with passion, from the heart. If you make mistakes, do not worry about it. Speeches almost never go exactly according to plan.

If you want to know how important these four steps are, think about what will happen if you don't do them. If you don't:

1// Know your audience; you'll have to guess what the audience wants.

2// Outline; you'll have to make up the content on the spot.

3// Rehearse; you'll have to improvise the delivery.

4// Speak with passion; you'll have to fake enthusiasm and interest.

Would anyone want to listen to a speech like that?

Written Communication

Another key part of persuasive communication is knowing how to write professionally. When you start working some day, your employer may require you to do an on-the-spot writing test before giving you a job. If you consistently send typo-filled emails or cannot communicate well with customers, you may receive a poor performance evaluation or even lose your job.

Here are some key things you can do starting now to improve your writing:

Assignments // Take every written assignment you get seriously, especially big papers.

Journal // Write in a journal several times a week. You can write about anything that interests you — your activities, special events, or your feelings.

Read // Trying to be a good writer without being a good reader is like trying to be a good hockey player without knowing how to ice skate. The more you read, the better you will write.

Take a course // Take all the writing classes you can.

Practice being professional // Whenever you email an adult, use proper grammar and write in letter format, starting with a "Dear ____"

Read books about writing // *Elements of Style* by Strunk and White is a classic. Many writers recommend reading it once every year. The book is now available online for free. Another great book to read is *On Writing* by the famous writer Stephen King.

If you look at the list above carefully, you will see that writing requires practice. It's pretty simple. To write better, write more.

Applying Persuasion

Now that you have had a chance to think about Persuasion, look at the following questions and reflect on the answers. Use your responses to figure out how you can improve your ability to persuade.

//   Which of the tools of persuasion come easiest to you?
     Are you good at telling stories? At using numbers? At
     understanding the needs of others? Which tools of
     persuasion do you need to develop?
//   Are there any opportunities for you to practice your public
     speaking skills in the next month?
//   How could you improve your writing skills in the next
     month? Can you try extra hard on your writing assignments,
     ask your teacher for feedback, read books about writing,
     or practice writing in your journal?

// FLEXIBILITY

Fifty years ago, it was common for someone to start and end his/her career at the same company. Someone could start working at General Motors at age 22 and finish at General Motors at age 62.

Today, people switch jobs every three years on average. This means that every three years, adults find new jobs, get used to new bosses, learn to work with new colleagues, and sometimes learn completely new skills.

Of course, work isn't the only place where things change. Relationships change when people break up with boyfriends or girlfriends. Education changes when people start new classes and adjust to new teachers. Life changes when people go off to college, join the army, or move across the country.

Change is inevitable. Flexibility is your ability to handle change. It's your ability to land on your feet, to read and understand new situations quickly, and to move on after your life suddenly shifts. Sometimes you will seek out the change yourself, such as when you decide to try out for a sports team or audition for a play. Other times life will bring change to you, such as when your parents decide to move your family to a new town.

Regardless of how change comes about, you can increase your ability to navigate it successfully.

Stuck-Points

Ever since Jen was six, she loved theatre. By the time she was fifteen, she had been in over twenty-five plays.

86

Now, Jen is excited because her favorite play, Fiddler on the Roof, is her high school's spring theatrical production. She rehearses for weeks in preparation. Everything seems to go well at tryouts but then, inexplicably, Jen doesn't make the play. Not only does she not get the lead part, she's not chosen for any role. Have you ever had a disappointment like Jen's in your life? Have you ever been cut from a team, passed over for an opportunity, or missed out on something you really wanted?

Times like these are called **Stuck-Points**™. We're stuck thinking about what went wrong, our disappointment, and how we were ripped off. We're stuck thinking:

> "This cannot be happening."
> "I'm so mad I could…."
> "I'm just going to stay in my room and sulk for the next few weeks."
> "There's no way I can EVER be happy again."

John was supposed to go to his senior prom with his dream date, Heather. But two days before the prom, Heather changed her mind. She decided she didn't want to go with John anymore.

John was so mad he went outside that night and ran eleven miles in the rain. But when he came back home, he didn't feel any better. He was stuck, and didn't know how to get unstuck.

No matter your skin color or how much money you have, you will experience Stuck-Points™. Many times you will know you are at a Stuck-Point but you will not know how to get yourself "unstuck."

Sometimes you will be so furious you don't even want to think about getting "unstuck." But eventually, you will have to find a way out. Otherwise, you'll be stuck forever.

If you have a high level of Flexibility you can get unstuck from most challenges quickly. If you lack Flexibility, thirty years from now, you'll still be talking about the time that drama teacher cut you from Fiddler on the Roof.

How to get "Unstuck"

To understand how to get unstuck, imagine you are driving a car when it suddenly dies. You try to start the car again and it won't start. You get out, open the hood, and can't figure out what's wrong.

You can keep turning the key, hoping that the car will start, or you can say, "I'm stuck." Believe it or not, the first step in getting unstuck is simply recognizing that you're stuck.

If you're furious about getting cut from the school play, start by acknowledging the feeling. Go ahead and say, "I'm stuck. I'm really upset about this."

Once you know you're stuck, you can do the following things to get unstuck:

1// Take a moment to think.

Sometimes, just taking a moment to think and look around can solve your problem. For example, what if the car is just out of gas? By calming down to think, you can often see a simple solution.

2// **Ask for help.**

We all like our independence, but the reality is that everyone needs helps sometimes. No matter how smart or mature you are, you will need help at some point. Even the greatest athletes in the world get help from dozens of people in order to become the greatest. They are supported by their coaches, trainers and nutritionists.

If your car is stuck, you can call for a tow truck. Or you can call your mom or dad. Or you can look around to see if there's anyone nearby who's willing to push the car. Or you can call a repair shop.

Please keep in mind that some Stuck-Points™ are so serious that you should absolutely get help no matter what. If you're depressed, have an eating disorder, a drug addiction, or problems with the law, or if you are the victim of abuse, get help immediately. You may not want to seek assistance because you don't think anyone can help you or you are worried about the consequences. But get the help. There are some things we simply cannot conquer on our own. Or maybe we can struggle with them on our own, but fixing the situation is slow, painful, and ineffective.

3// **Focus on solutions.**

When you are stuck, all you can see is the problem. To get unstuck, focus on solutions.

Solutions for your car trouble can include walking home and picking the car up later, or taking a bus or train home if you're in a big city.

Or, you can keep thinking about the problem without actually trying to solve it. If you take this approach, you can:

// Get mad and kick the car.
// Curse at the crummy person who ripped you off and sold you a bad car.
// Think of all the bad things that have happened that day.

Focus on the problem or focus on the solution – that's your choice. People who get unstuck fast spend 80% of their time on the solution, and 20% on the problem.

If you get cut from a team, play another sport. If your best friend abandons you, find another one. If you don't get into your dream college, get excited about a different college. If your girlfriend dumps you, remind yourself that there are three billion other people you can date, even if it's hard for you to believe at that moment.

4// **Turn a negative into a positive.**
Ask yourself, "Is there any way that I can turn this negative into a positive?"

For example, how might you turn this negative car situation into a positive? Can you use the situation to learn more about cars? Can you motivate yourself to work hard and save money for a reliable car? Can you invite your best friends to help you and create a legendary memory about the time you all pushed the car? Jen, after getting cut from the theatre group, could have contacted everyone else who got cut and put together their own play.

You may not be able to control what happens to you, but you can control how you react. You can choose to find a positive in a negative.

5// **Use contrast.**

By comparing your situation to a much more challenging one, you might realize that you're actually pretty lucky.

For example, in the car example, you could remind yourself that there are many people in the world who will never have the chance to drive a car. You could think of all the people who live in oppressive countries, where you might be tortured just for having an opinion different from the dictator's.

Then you'd think, "Wow! I'm lucky to be here, stuck on the side of the road with this car. At least I have a car to drive. For most of history, people had to ride horses around town."

Learning to make our challenges and disappointments small is an important part of getting unstuck. Instead of turning one disappointment into the end of the world, we can say, "NEXT! I'm choosing to get unstuck."

6// **Change your environment.**

Sometimes we get stuck because of our environment. Every time we hang out with certain people, we get in trouble. Every time we sit down to do our homework, we watch TV instead. To get unstuck, you can't just try harder; you have to do something differently. For example, you might have to study in a room without a TV. In other words, you have to change your environment.

If a problem is big enough, and there are no good alternatives, you might even need to switch sports, classes, or even schools.

In the car example, you might notice that your car gets stuck anytime you drive on bumpy roads. Perhaps you should only drive on paved roads. Or maybe you need to buy a new car.

7// **Give yourself time.**

Finally, you can give yourself time. Tell yourself, "I'm really upset and disappointed right now, but things will get better." Or, "I'm crushed right now, but I believe that I'll find a way to be happy again." It's natural and normal to be upset when something bad happens, so you don't have to act like you're not upset. You just want to monitor yourself and make sure you don't stay stuck for too long.

Giving yourself time is particularly important for devastating Stuck-Points™ such as losing a loved one. During really tough times, you'll definitely want to ask for help, and review your entire list of options for getting unstuck.

Flexibility is your ability to get unstuck when confronted with problems and challenges. You learned seven ways to get unstuck. Here's an opportunity to review what you've learned:

1// Take a moment to think.
2// Ask for help.
3// Focus on solutions.
4// Turn the negative into a positive.
5// Use contrast to make yourself feel better.
6// Change your environment.
7// Give yourself time.

Examples

Now read the descriptions written below. How would you get unstuck in the following situations?

Lose your starting position

You were the starting shortstop on your softball team and then an All-State shortstop moves to your area. She takes your starting position.

Friendship changes

Colin was your best friend all through middle school. You played football together after school; you went over to each other's houses at least once a week; and you ate lunch together most days.

Now in 9th grade, he joined the football team, but you didn't. You don't have any of the same classes. You greet each other in the hallways but you are not close friends anymore. You miss him.

Relationship problems

You've been dating Amanda for two years, but she breaks up with you. She's dating someone else at school and you see them together all the time. You're devastated and embarrassed and it's all you can think about.

Stuck with friends

Sam had five best friends who had all been to jail. Sam didn't want to go to jail, but they kept coming over to his house every day, asking him to hang out, and he found it hard to say no every time. But every time he hung out with them, he risked that they would do something that got him in trouble.

Rejection from a college

You've always dreamed of going to Florida State, but you are denied admission.

Applying Flexibility

Now that you have had a chance to think about Flexibility, look at the following questions and reflect on the answers. Use your responses to figure out how you can increase your Flexibility.

// Think of a time in your life when you were stuck? What did it take to get unstuck?

// What is one Stuck-Point in your life right now that you can address?

// When you face a problem, do you spend 80% of your energy on the problem or 80% the solution? Are you somewhere in between?

Solution Power Summary

Your Solution Power consists of three things:

// Creativity: The ability to create new solutions.

// Persuasion: Using communication to gain support.

// Flexibility: The ability to adjust to change.

If you have low Solution Power, you will limit yourself to existing options, fail to get support when you need it, and stay stuck when facing change or challenges.

If you have high Solution Power, you will find novel ways to win, convince others to support you, and adjust quickly to new situations.

Conclusion

We started this book with the stories of Paul and Mandy. Let's finish with two more true stories.

Kyle is sixteen years old and lives in a group home. He has never met his father and his mother is in prison for the next twelve years. At school, Kyle struggles with his classes and has few friends.

If you asked Kyle his biggest problem, he'd tell you, "I wish I knew my parents."

One day, Kyle did something small. Kyle pulled out a piece of paper and wrote a letter to his mother. He told her about his group home, his school, and how he missed her.

The days passed by. He didn't hear anything back.

And then Kyle got a letter back from his mother. She told him about her life in prison and encouraged Kyle to create a different life for himself.

Kyle wrote her again. And his mom wrote back. Dozens of letters later, Kyle had a relationship with his mother.

What's the point of this story? Kyle took action. He did something.

If you want a better life, take action. No action is too small - even your smallest action can have important consequences. So don't just read *The Success GPA*, apply it.

The Final Story

You already know the person in the final story. It's you. Just like Kyle, Paul, Mandy and everyone else you read about in this book, you have a story. Every day, you choose what kind of story you will have.

Every time you take action to stay in the Lasting Zone, you're building your Awareness Power. Even the smallest act of Service builds your Social Power. Each time you say "Yes and…" you build your Solution Power.

As you build your Success GPA, you'll also see how to combine your different powers. For example, when you face a problem, you can:

// Ask yourself the question: "How can I solve this problem?" By asking this question, you're using Awareness Power (asking good questions to control your Focus), and Solution Power (Using your Flexibility to focus 80% on the solution and 20% on the problem).

// Use your Social Power to ask three different people how they'd solve the problem (tapping your network Diversity), and then if you know your personality type is Explorer, you can check yourself to ensure you're not being impulsive (Awareness Power).

Little by little, action after action, as you build your Success GPA™ powers, you will get stronger until you can do things you previously considered impossible.

But you'll miss out on all this growth if you only focus on your grades. While Math, Science, and English classes are important, they're only half the story. When you develop your Success GPA™, you give yourself a whole new way to win.

If you want to measure your Success GPA™, and learn how to increase your chances of getting good jobs, expanded social opportunities and more, visit SuccessGPA.com

About the Author

Mawi Asgedom has written eight books that are used in thousands of classrooms across North America. He has spoken to more than one million students and educators in more than 40 states, and is the founder of Mental Karate.

As a child, Mawi fled civil war in Ethiopia and survived a Sudanese refugee camp. After immigrating to the U.S., he overcame many challenges to graduate from Harvard University.

Mawi's passion is to equip youth for lives of opportunity and fulfillment. He maintains a website at MawiSpeaks.com

Made in the USA
San Bernardino, CA
17 May 2017